What Would Caitlin Wear

A book by RL Lane

Dedicated to a Caitlin. Caitlin A. Not Caitlin B. or Caitlin C...

"It was the big question. We all wondered what she would wear…" RL Lane

Would it be a wild tango dress to sashay down the aisle? She is a lot of fun…

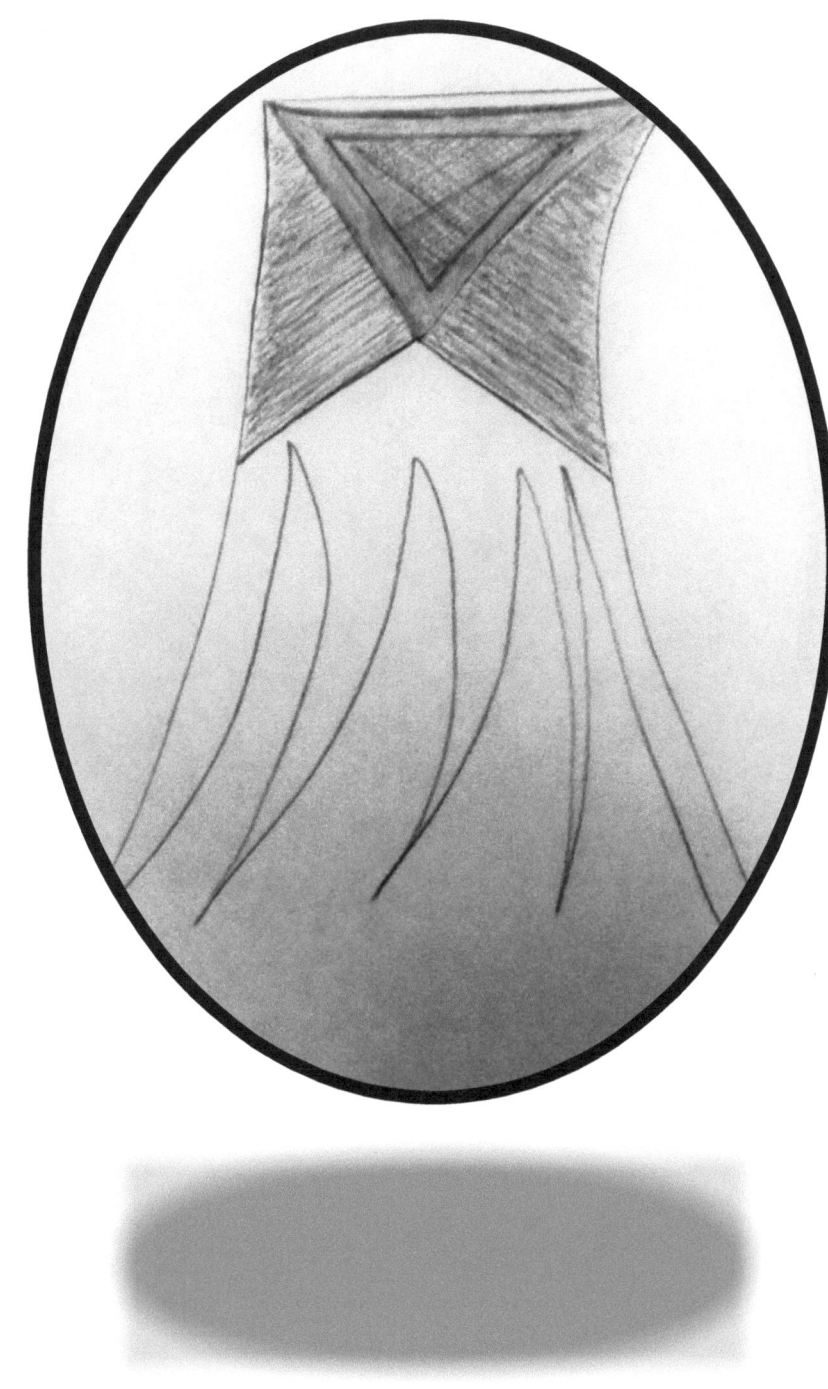

Would it be a long dress with ribbon and lace running down to the floor?

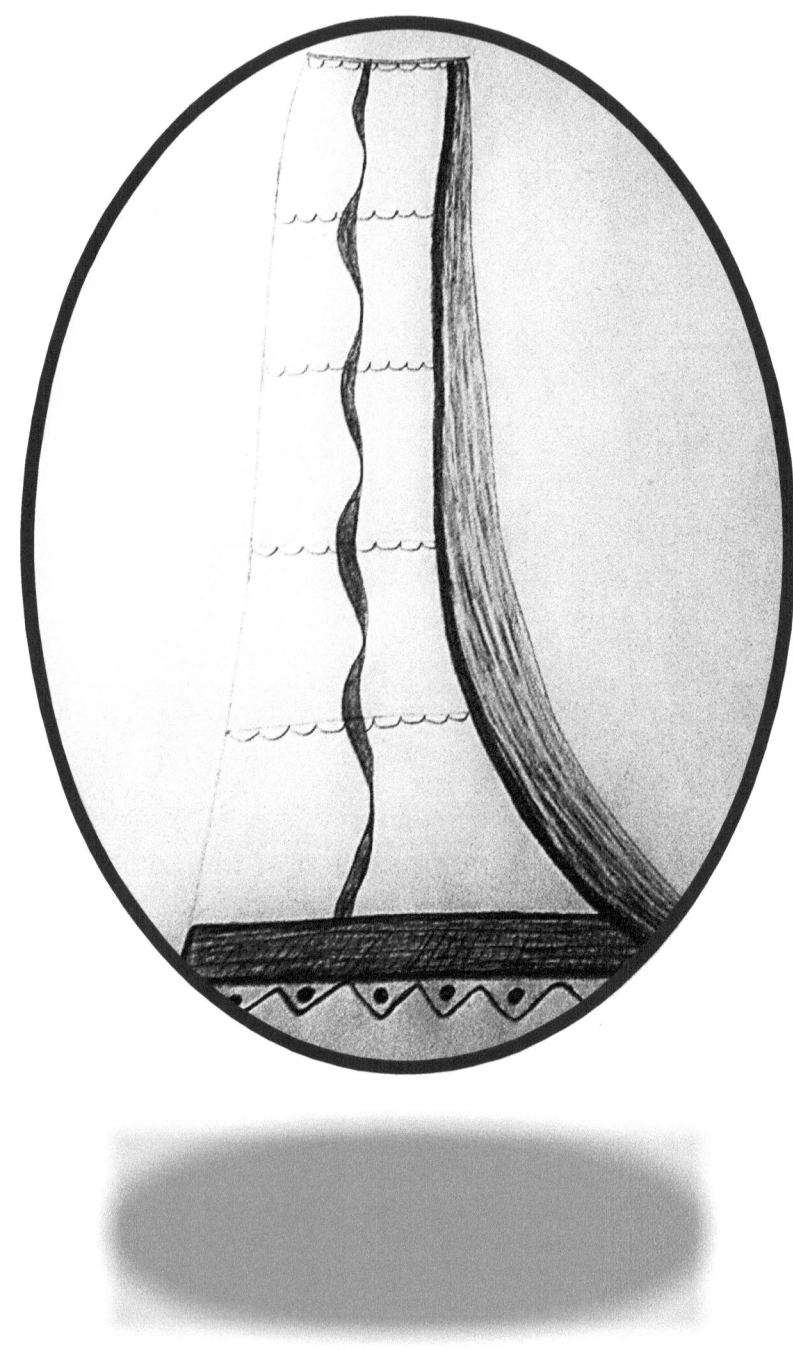

Would it be a "wedding cake dress"? Well surely that would be something different. The talk of all the town…

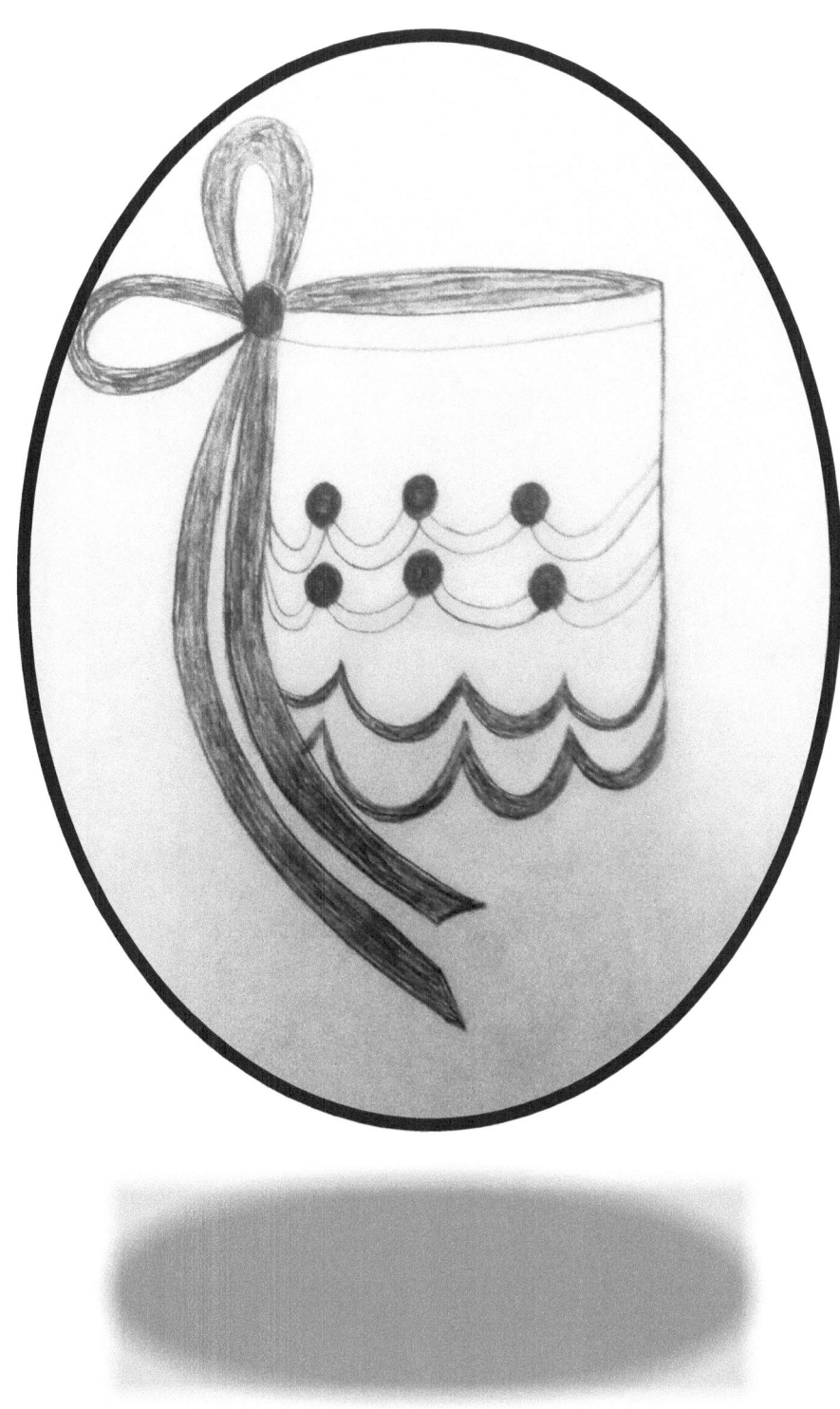

Would it be a bright pink bubble dress to match her bubbly personality? A soft and fluffy dress…

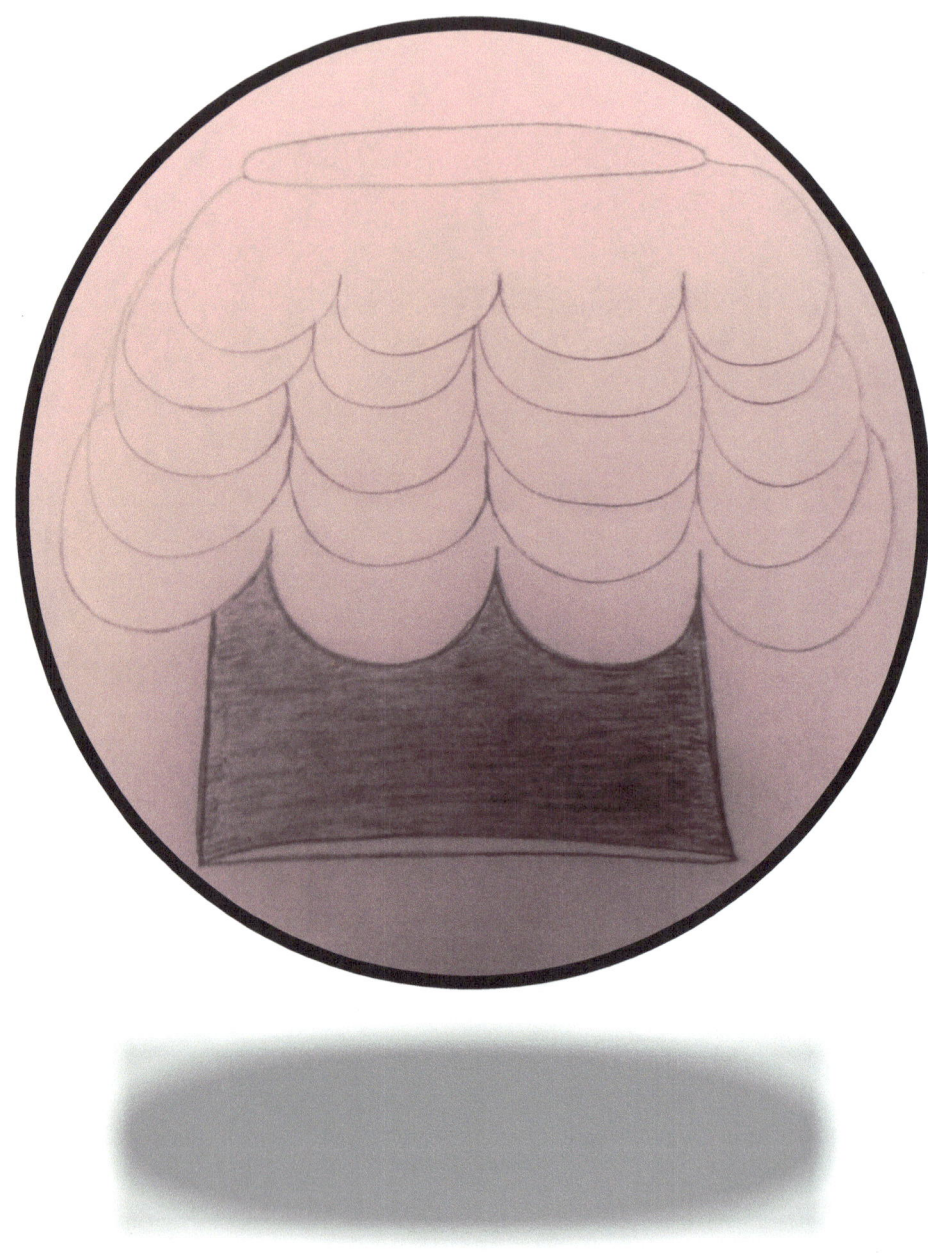

Regardless of what she wears, they will all be there. Her friends and family will watch her walk down…the ones who watched her grow up from…

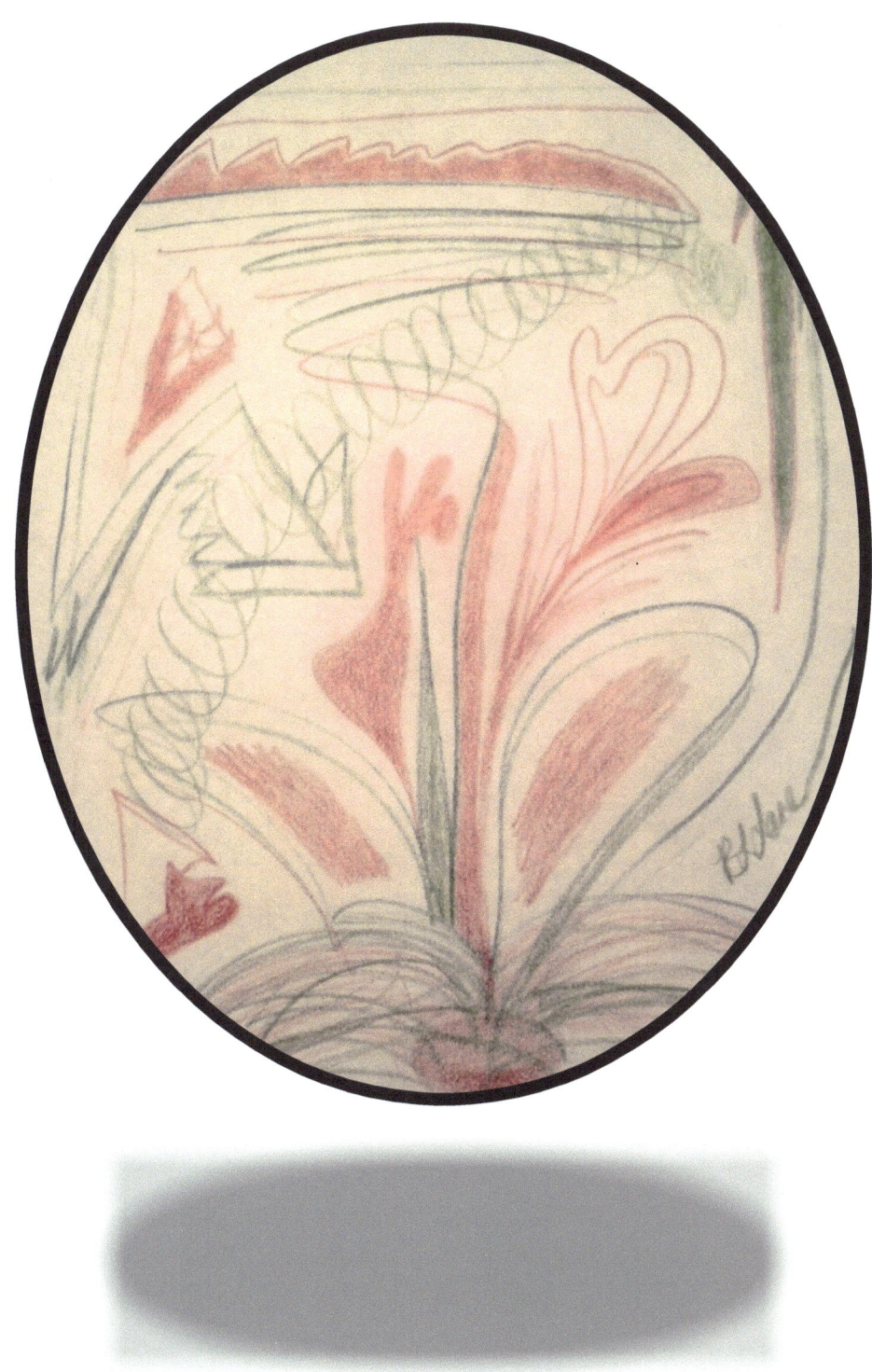

A little girl who loved her dolls

A little girl with big blue eyes

That would look all around

Within the sweetest face

She grew and grew

And then grew some more

Is she taller now than her Dad

I really am not sure

Many will remember the day she was first born

Many will remember

Looking down on her

Wishing her all the best

Only life's best for the little girl

The one they named…

Caitlin.

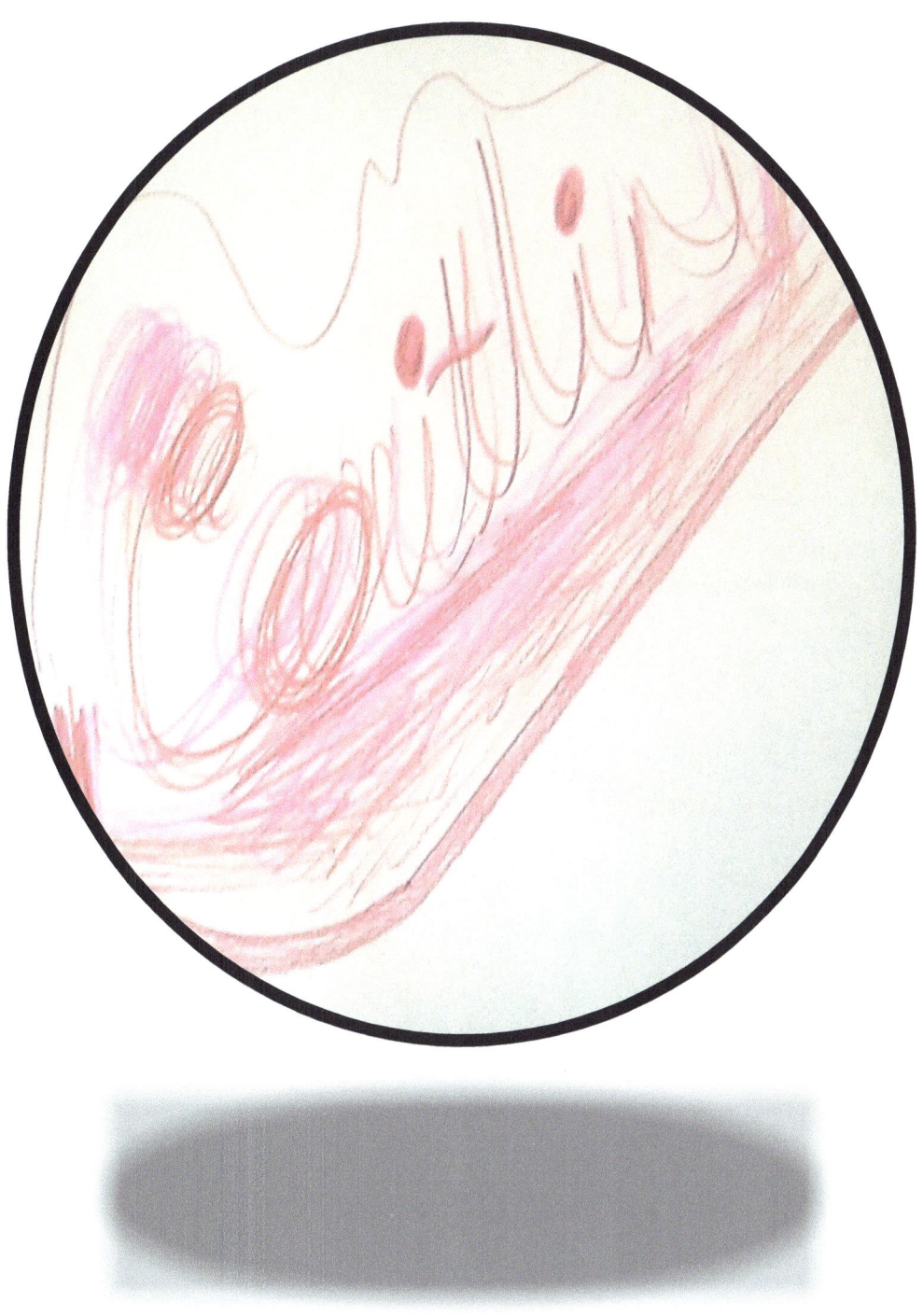

I don't actually know what her name means. I don't really need to know what it means because she defined it for herself.

She defined it to be someone who cares. Just ask her cat. He is probably busy resting his head on a pillow, dreaming of his next dinner.

Oh. The dreams.

Remember the dreams.

Remember to follow them.

That is why we have them…so we can follow them.

Well, her wedding is not at Christmas time, so I don't think she'll be wearing this…

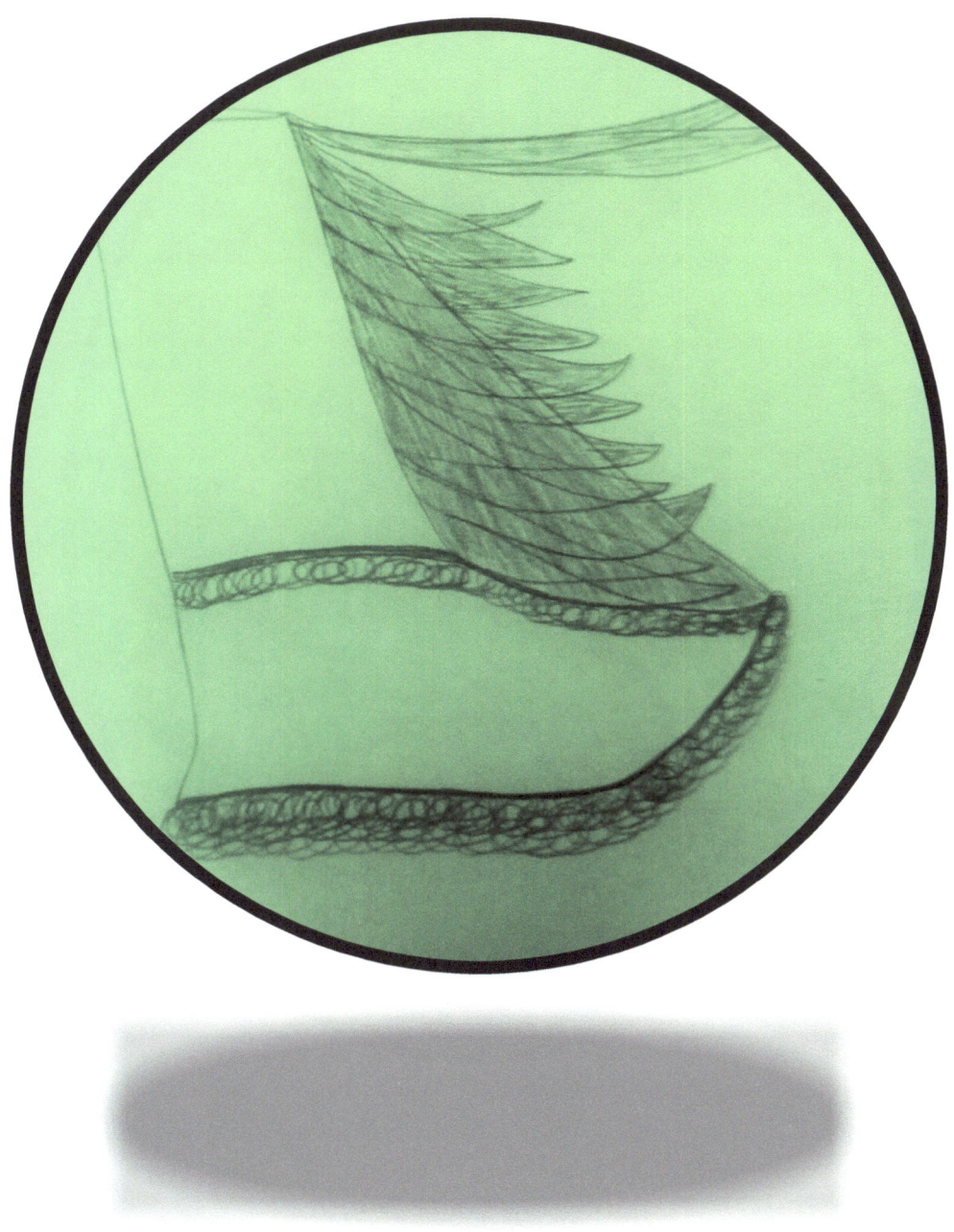

I doubt the back of her dress will have this kind of train…

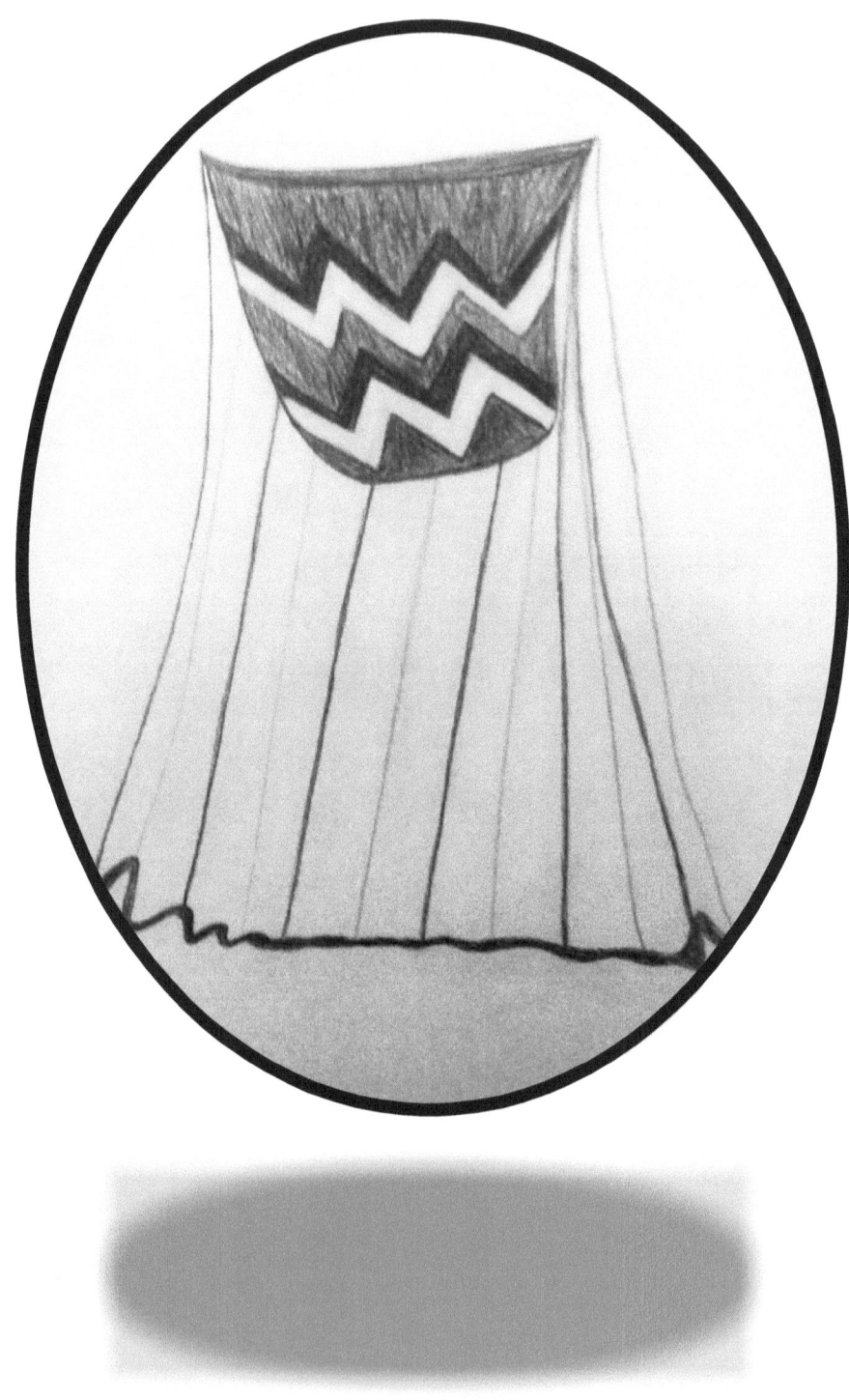

If she wears a "deep romance" dress it'll remind her to look deep in her mate's eyes as she waltzes around the floor…

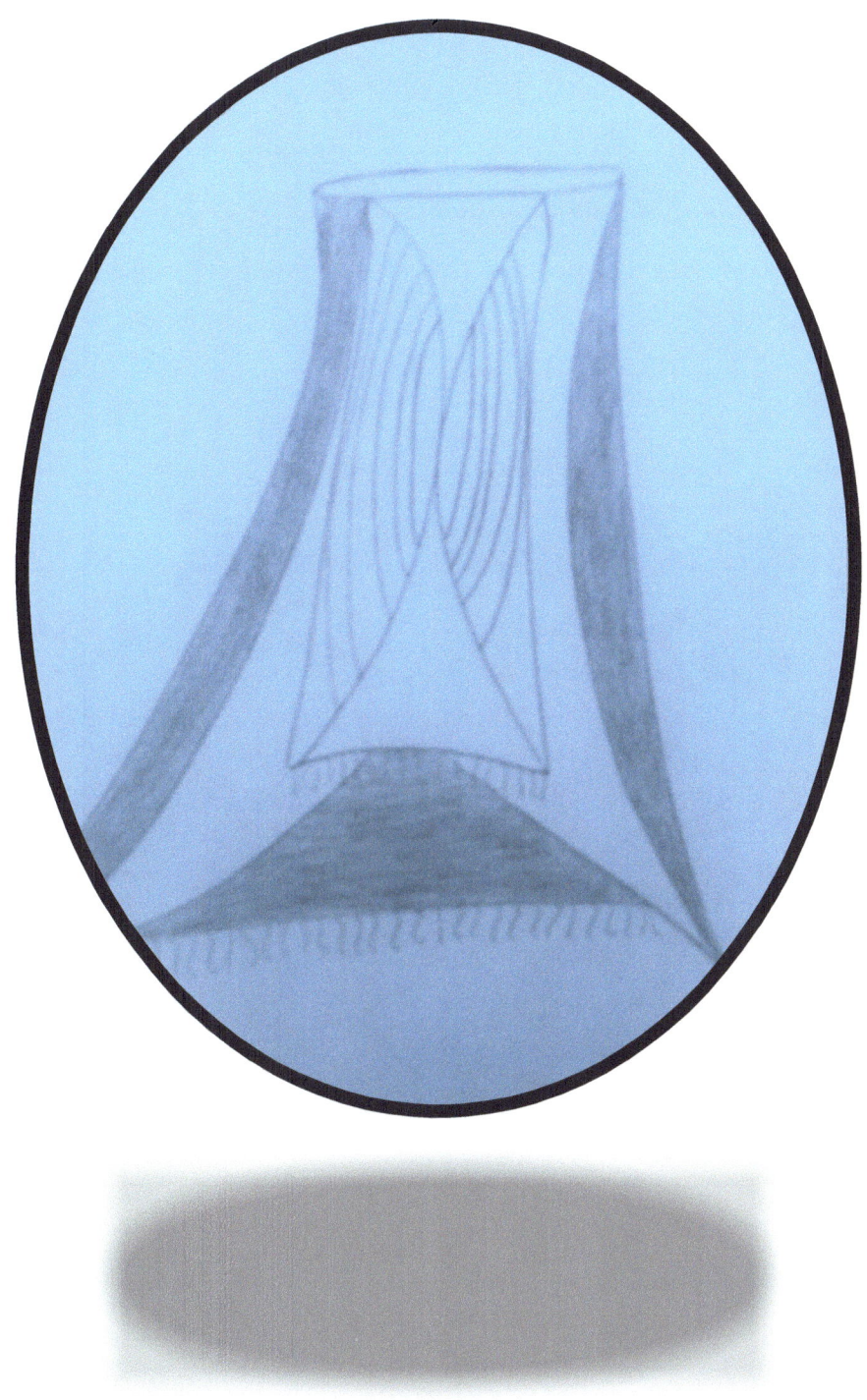

If RL Lane could design her dress, I would make her a long elegant dress that slightly sparkles. A dress that fits her perfectly. A beautifule beautifule dress to match

how beautifule she is.

On the inside.

How beautifule she is on the inside...

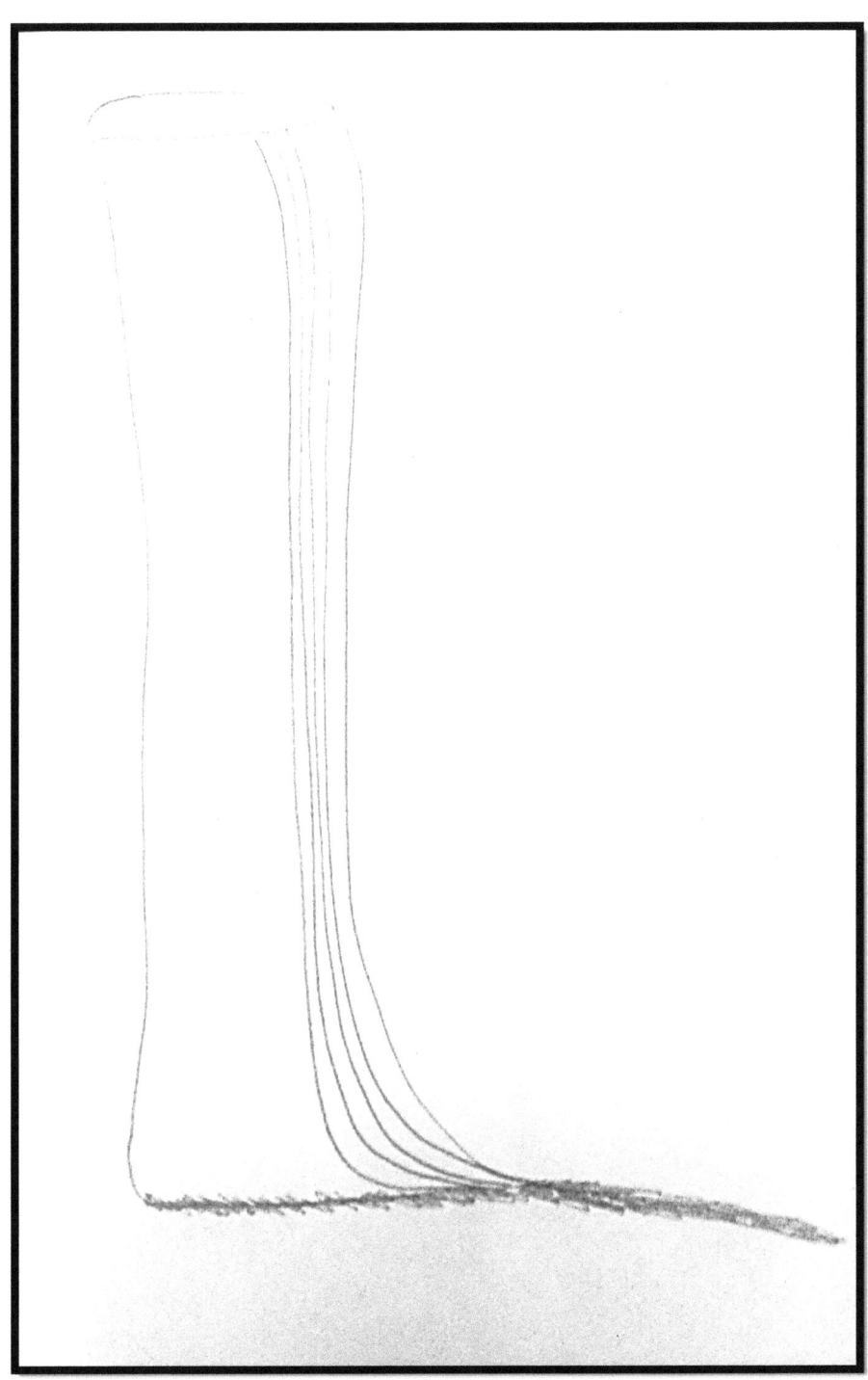

It won't matter where the ceremony takes place…rain or shine…the people will be there to see her…

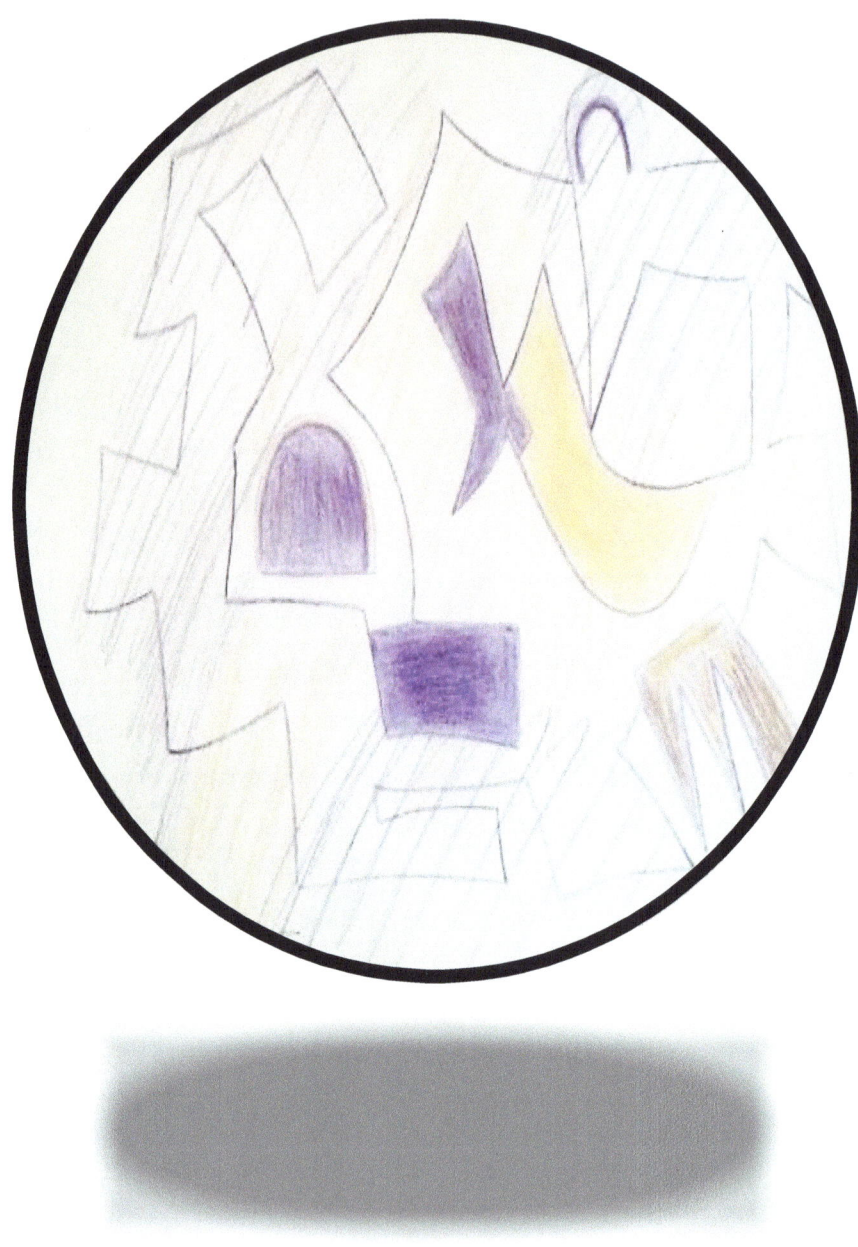

They will all wish her love forever…

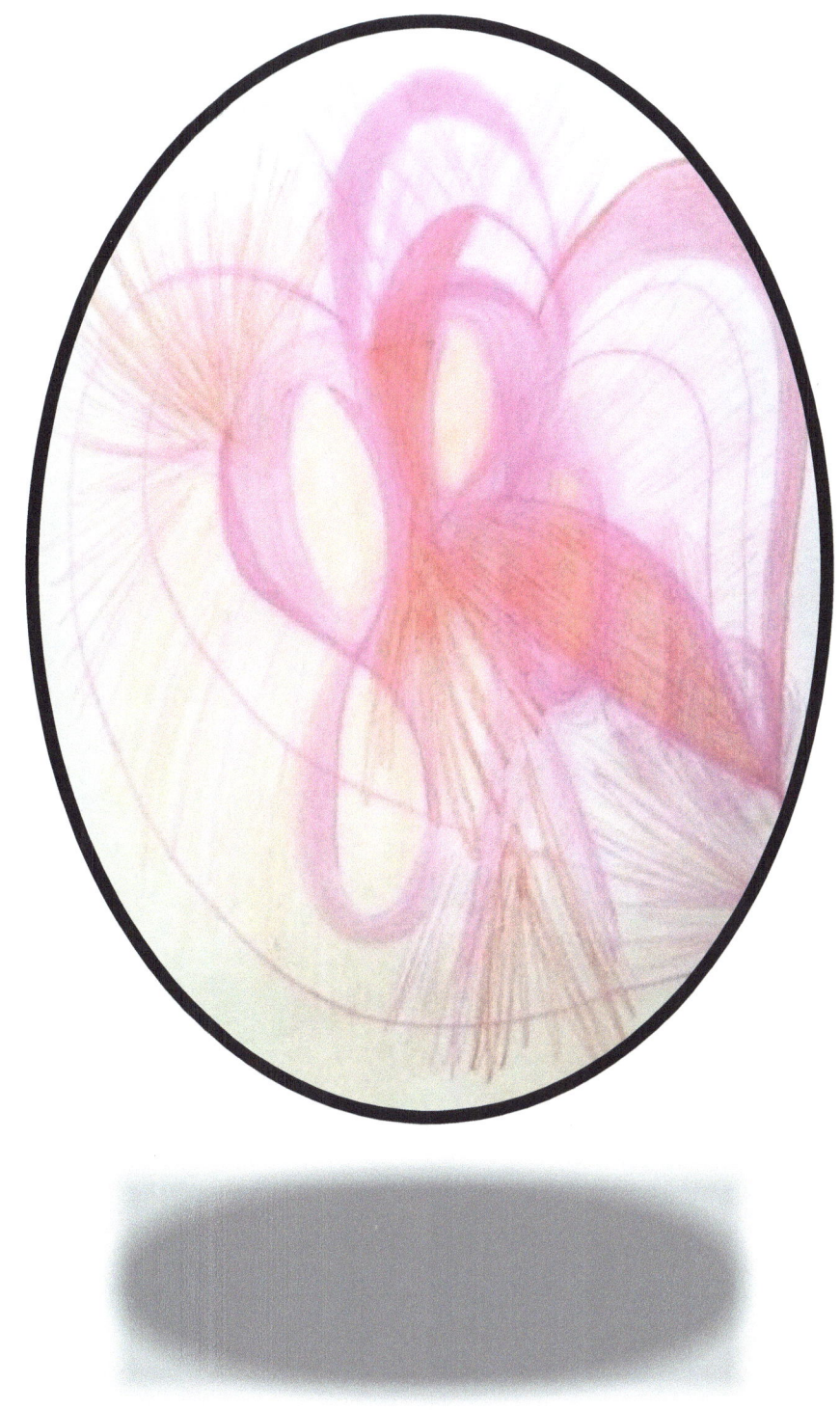

To all the little girls…the ones who grew up…

The first family…the one you were born into…

Will always be there for you…

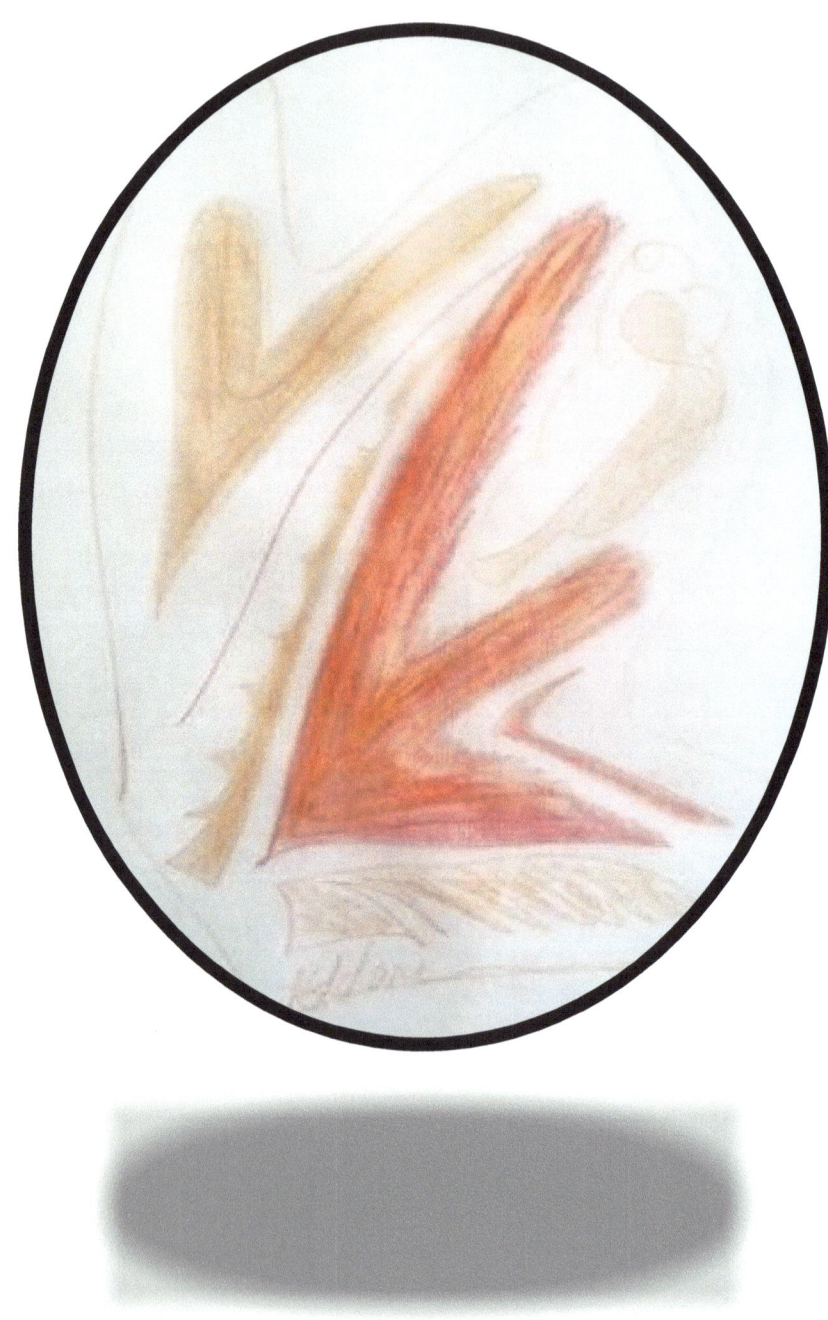

And remember the race…

> As the car turns the corner and the horse jumps over the line…

It doesn't matter how fast you get to the finish…

It doesn't matter how many paths you have to cross…

It just matters how much you loved along the way…

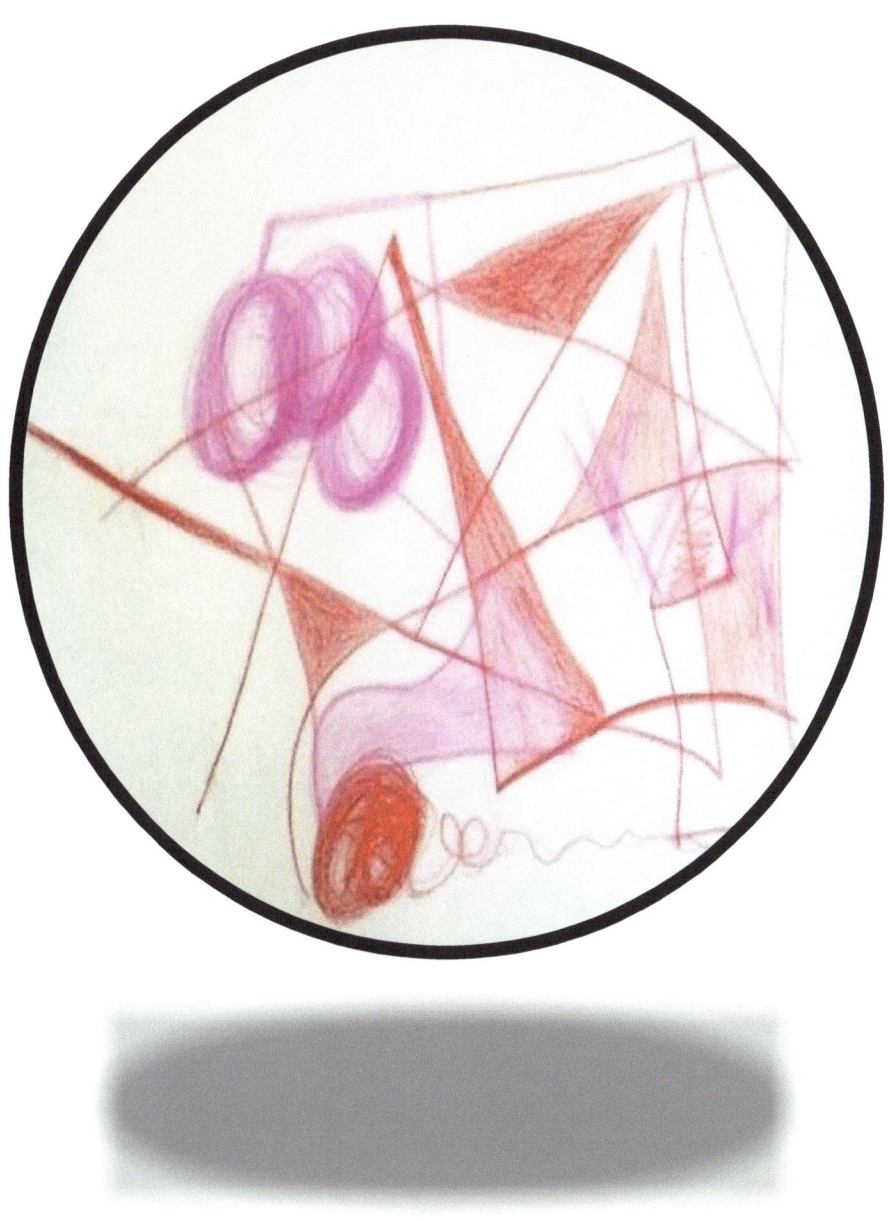

About the Author

RL Lane has published the EcarreT series and a collection of art books featuring the illustrations throughout the books. The series begins with "Chapel Street Signs"…

…unexplained connections that challenge us to beli ve. A woman, a Dad a Doctor, a cat and mouse, a horse and tale tell their stories. "Do you beli ve in spirits?" I asked my friend. "Well look", he said, "I believe there are things that cannot be explained…" Oh. Plus, hear ov a Mom's battle with her struggle to connect to the woman…her little girl.

Welcome to EcarreT…a world
Where everyone cares
Why did I have to create it in…

A fiction fantasy world?

You may already know why, but you will see regardless of what you believe as a girl's journey of love and faith on her "Touring Machine" take her on the best journey of her mundane life. A life well on its way takes a turn in a direction that could've never been seen or even dreamed…

The author can be contacted at:

RosaLeeeLane@gmail.com
www.Amazon.com/author/readrllane

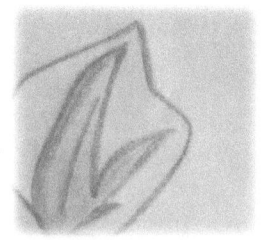

www.ingramcontent.com/pod-product-compliance
Lightning Source LLC
Chambersburg PA
CBHW050433180526
45159CB00006B/2521